EXTREME PROJECT MANAGEMENT

EXTREME PROJECT MANAGEMENT

Unique Methodologies – Resolute Principles – Astounding Results

Shaun Ajani

Writers Club Press

San Jose   New York   Lincoln   Shanghai

Extreme Project Management
Unique Methodologies – Resolute Principles – Astounding Results

Writers Club Press
an imprint of iUniverse, Inc.

For information address:
iUniverse, Inc.
5220 S. 16th St., Suite 200
Lincoln, NE 68512
www.iuniverse.com

ISBN: 0-595-21335-9

Printed in the United States of America

To
All the professionals, who always do things the hard
way . . .
Your time has come . . .

EPIGRAPH

"Without ambition one starts nothing. Without work one finishes nothing. The prize will not be sent to you. You have to win it. The man who knows how will always have a job. The man who also knows why will always be his boss. As to methods there may be a million and then some, but principles are few. The man who grasps principles can successfully select his own methods. The man who tries methods, ignoring principles, is sure to have trouble."

Ralph Waldo Emerson

"Companies and individual careers do not endure, unless one worships a certain amount of principles and values driven doctrine in the occupation. It is disturbing to note that this may be a pragmatic stipulation adopted by the profession more for economic obligations, rather then being an evolution in human virtues."

Shaun H. Ajani

CONTENTS

PREFACE

The Beginning

In the ancient times, people just harvested all the chores and responsibilities, which needed to be fulfilled in order to meet a final objective...And just did it. That was the "project". Then a few thousand years ago there was talk about some people, who actually broke down these jobs in tasks, and in fact used separate resources to accomplish these tasks. These were the brilliant people that hung out in the palaces with royalty. These were the Project Managers.

Were they any smarter? They probably were. Did they have access to better technology? Of course not, all they did was use a better version of the common sense, available at that time. But those who succeeded also had a most crucial ingredient, principle. A sort of responsibility and accountability for the people they attended to, primarily their masters. And those who succeeded, as well as survived, knew how to mix a certain sense of principle with the latest, and the most realistic, methodology available.

Certainly, times have changed. Companies and individual careers do not endure, unless one worships a certain amount of principles and values driven doctrine in the occupation. It is disturbing to note that this may be a pragmatic stipulation adopted by the profession more for economic obligations, due to competition, rather then being an evolution in human virtues. The good news is that with proper methodologies, it is unproblematic to follow this path.

Nevertheless, as time slithered along, common sense got refined and polished, resulting in "better technology". "Clients" replaced "masters", and "servants" gave way to "consultants". But beware, for these refined and polished common senses, in forms of ideas, methodologies, and theories *will either take you to the palace, or will get you thrown in the lion's pen.*

ACKNOWLEDGEMENTS

I would like to gratefully acknowledge the following companies for making this book possible:

Nation Gifts: For giving me a shot at using my writing and creativity in the corporate world

Code Factory LLC: For introducing me to the brilliance and creative methodology that every triumphant company must posses in the founding fathers

Dollar Stores Inc: For making me a leader, so I can see that perspective

Spherion: For throwing me out to the Fortune 500 companies, so I can use that perspective

———————▼———————

CHAPTER ONE

WHAT IS EXTREME PROJECT MANAGEMENT?

"Great spirits have always found violent opposition from mediocrity. The latter cannot understand it when a man does not thoughtlessly submit to hereditary prejudices but honestly and courageously uses his intelligence."—Albert Einstein

One can study the methodology and become a professional ahead of one's time. But there are some consequences that will come along with the territory. There will always be people, who will not understand, or will simply be behind the times. They will be unfamiliar with your methods, and will be afraid of you. Afraid sounds like a strong word, but in essence they will fear, what they do not comprehend. And in their haste of goodwill to "set things straight", they may inadvertently sabotage your efficiency.

In a nutshell, you will encounter three kinds of people, the Unapprised, the Sanctimonious, and the Open Leader.

The Unapprised person will be the biggest threat. This person will, due to being uninformed and somewhat imprudent, not understand the complex interdependencies of the several methodologies of the Extreme Project Manager (EPM). And will either be a hindrance in the big picture, or just downright insubordinate.

The Sanctimonious will understand the value of the end result, but will have a problem with the means of deployment, as Extreme Project Management has some effective, yet revolutionary modus operandi. Hence, the Sanctimonious will try and implement a self-governing and self-righteous remedy to neutralize any possible threat to his sense of regulatory order. The Sanctimonious, unlike the uninformed, can be converted to the Open Leader.

The Open Leader will have an engaging attitude toward emerging methodologies, which can benefit the project. If the EPM is new to the organization, or does not yet enjoy a position of suitable authority, the Open Leader can be a wonderful conduit to deploy the Extreme Project Management.

Extreme Project Management

We have come a long way, but we still primarily do the projects in the same manner. And keeping in line with the 'polishing of the common sense' model, evolved my Extreme Project Management.

The system is screaming for managers that meet the profile of an Extreme Project Manager. Extreme Project Management is a methodology, bordering on tactical operations of an ongoing project, which results in the completion of the project ahead of a normal timeline, at the same time adorning and embellishing the status of the Project Manager, in the eyes of the client, or the project stakeholder. Truly a win-win situation, where the client gets a tremendous package for the money, and the Project Manager keeps flying upwards on the career ladder.

This is accomplished by performing all the duties and tasks of the Project Manager at a super heightened level. The proper Project Methodology must be followed. However, it is properly tuned to produce the phenomenal end results. It will be valuable to demonstrate a brief and cursory summarization of the Extreme Project Management methodology.

Meeting

Most Project Managers do not consider it, but the first phase of any management methodology begins from the initial meeting with the client, or the project stakeholders. In this meeting, you must establish yourself as the expert; in whatever that ails the client. Monitor the client closely to observe how he is reacting to your body language, adjust accordingly, but do not try and over interpret the client's body language. Ensure that you close robustly by asking for the project to be given to you, and eradicate any chances the competition may have over you.

Analysis

Before beginning the operations of any project, proper analysis must be performed. The Extreme Project Manager must always keep in mind that the analysis is actually a way to accentuate the value being provided to the client, by exactly spelling out what benefits the clients will gain, once the project is over. For example, if the project is about creating a new Content Management System (CMS), then the client must be made aware, in writing, how the new CMS will improve the organization.

The Extreme Analysis for Extreme Project Management is also about breaking down the project in big easily digestible chunks, where the client can see in one shot, how the phases of the project will be laid out. This is not the same as the Work Breakdown Structure (WBS), Critical Path Method (CPM), and Project Evaluation Review Technique (PERT), which are more detailed. Although, not as detailed in Extreme Project Management.

Project Management Process

During the day-to-day operations of Project Management, there are many aspects of Extreme Project Management, which can achieve the two main objectives. When I say, day-to-day, I mean normal operational responsibilities of the Project Manager, like meetings, dealings with the project staff, and other more detailed aspects, such as Quality Assurance, Risk Analysis, and creating a new infrastructure for future Project Managers for the client.

For example, an Extreme Project Manager can improve on meetings by employing such novel techniques like, the two-sided meeting and Time/Importance Framing (TIF). An Extreme Project Manager can also install new and improved heavily delegated methodologies for functions, such as Defect Tracking, Risk Equalizer, and the creation of appropriate forms and documents.

Each of the exact methodology for Extreme Project Management described has been designed with the ultimate objectives in mind, which are the completion of the project ahead of a normal timeline, and the magnified respect of the Project Manager, in the eyes of the client.

CHAPTER TWO

▼

IMPRESSIONS

You have heard all the clichés about first impressions. And they are all true. However, the first meeting with the client is not just about first impressions, but also more about impressing upon the client how significant you can be to the project, and closing the deal before leaving the meeting place. From the way you present your place in the industry, to the words you say to close the deal, all come together for the successful first meeting.

Rank

Chances are that the client has never heard of you, when you first walk in. You must establish yourself immediately. The reason behind this is simple. We have all grown up, regardless of culture or country, in environments governed by rank and structure. Give yourself a rank; it is an automatic extra point.

Announce your rank in the industry to the client. If you don't have a special degree like 'Doctor of something', have a rank of some kind. If you are independent or have your own company, then it is easy. Announce yourself as the director, or the Vice President of a department. If you work for a major firm, and do not have an impressive title yet, then use anything that defines you. For example, introduce yourself as, "Hi, I am Shaun Ajani, Project Manager" (it will be more effective if you use your own name here).

Expert

Nothing is sweeter to a client then hearing that you are an expert at something they desperately need solved. One good thing about being a Project Manager is that you do not have to be an expert particularly at anything specific, just Project Management. As a skilled Extreme Project Manager, you will pick out the expert people, who will populate your project.

Declaring yourself an expert to the client is simple. First, just ask the right questions to determine exactly what the client needs help with. Second, make a mental note to pick the right person on your team, or if the client is assigning the team, ensure that you specifically ask for that particular skill. Make a point to remind the client that it is a crucial skill. And third, quickly mention to the client a past experience and client, even if it is not exactly the same circumstance, where you successfully collaborated to solve a similar problem. The client does not want you to be the lone expert, just give the image that you will solve the problem.

The professional world is besieged with people, who declare themselves as an expert in something. And if this is carried out with enough self-assurance, the mass will believe it. Just walk into any bookstore and you will be inundated with books, tapes, and videos of these experts introducing new programs and courses. When enough faith is put in these experts, changes do happen. Hence, it is not the actual ability and the skills of the expert, but of the person receiving it.

Your objective is to deliver this image in such a way that the client, or your audience, will put their trust in you. The great thing about this is that with the right staff and little knowledge, you can pull this off successfully. Follow the three steps outlined above in this chapter and do some research, before you meet with the client.

Once you have established yourself as the expert, usually after a few weeks at the client site, you may have the option of furthering yourself in the field, or just move onto something else. That's the great advantage of this Expert methodology. The benefits are staggering. You can easily write an article or two, just by being exposed to a new technique or a methodology at a client site. Or you can simply apply the new lessons you learned at another client site, thus establishing yourself as the expert with even more confidence. Or further still, just pick another topic that interests you, and move on.

Always keep yourself open to new ideas, even if they have intimated you before. For example, I was always anxious about not being able to do programming. But after reading a few books, I can easily function within any group that deploys complex programming in the project. I started out by reading some simple books about C++ programming. Knowing that it was not a matter of life or death, I never forced myself to memorize anything, all I did was just read.

Sometimes that is all it takes. Once you are exposed to new ideas, techniques, and resources, you will automatically be able to function. Remember, as the Project Manager, you are not required to actually perform the task itself, just be able to have an abstract understanding of it.

During any project, where you declare yourself as the expert, do not let the client strong-arm you in performing menial tasks. As an effective EPM you will need to deploy a lot of the methodologies of the EPM, and covering each little task, as defined in your Work Breakdown Structure, must not inundate you.

The same goes for your team members, it is important to remember that there will always be many team members, who will be more knowledgeable about a subject than you are. Do not let that intimidate you. The ruse is to project the same expert image, at the same time be able to use the team member's expertise for the advantage of the project. It is acceptable to disclose to the team member that your expertise lies in more of an abstract form, needed to run the project. However, there may be certain tasks that will need the "particular expertise" of that team member.

Sir Isaac Newton once said, "If I have seen further it is by standing on the shoulders of giants." Use the opportunity of having people smarter then you on the team to further yourself. You do not have to be the best in everything. In fact, if you try to project that image, your own team members will quickly mark you as a fake, and you will be less effective for you client.

Body Language

I have to admit, I am not a very big believer in body language. I know that it differs vastly from culture to culture, and from country to country. That is exactly why you need to be aware of body language. There are basically two things to consider here, how *not* to misinterpret body language, and how *not* to be misunderstood.

A few years ago, I had the unfortunate opportunity of being taken into for questioning by some very sinister looking Russian officials, at a Russian airport. I was the only American flying from a small airport in Moscow to Alaska, and some unscrupulous Russian officials had picked me out. I sat in a barely furnished room. I did not speak a word of Russian (except being able to ask for the bathroom) and they did not speak a word of English. All they said was, 'problem!' and all I kept repeating was, 'no, no problem'. All I could see was four Russian guards in uniform looking at me, and talking amongst themselves in serious tones. By reading their body language I could *tell* that they wanted something *big* from me. And after hearing a lot of stories from other travelers, I knew it was money.

They were able to locate a Bulgarian, who spoke English. He exchanged a few words with the Russians for a while, and as I had suspected, he indicated that they knew that I lived in San Francisco, and was carrying US Dollars. I was carrying around $600, and would have gladly shared it with them. Except for one thing, I do not offer bribes, and I certainly was not going to be strong-armed into it. I *assumed* that the Russians had read that in *my* body language, and were determined to break me, especially with my flight leaving within the hour. Finally, the Bulgarian told me the amount the Russians were demanding. It was $25!

$25 between the four of them!

Do you see what happened here? I was reading their body language quite correctly, in a traditional body language way, by seeing that they were quite serious about acquiring something *awfully precious* from me. And at the same time, they read me quite correctly, again in a traditional body language manner...that I was not going to part with anything significant. Hence, as I mentioned earlier, there are two basic things to consider here, how *not* to misinterpret body language, and how *not* to be misunderstood. If I had considered that, and not relied on the Russians body language for a message, I might have appeared to be relaxed and 'willing to share'.

I learned a very valuable lesson that day. I never study the client for the traditional signs anymore. I do not care, whether the client is folding his arms, or scratching his nose, or looking out the window. I do not try and 'model' after the client to force a rapport.

I just make entirely sure that I appear neutral and interested.

For example, I always sit close to the table, slightly leaning forward, with both my arms on the table, either taking notes or slightly touching my hands at the figure tips. Look directly at the client, and nod occasionally, and you will be amazed, how well the meeting will go.

Close

Never leave the site of a meeting, before closing. Here's the one-two punch formula. First you must prep the client with an anticipatory question. I purchased a new car recently, and I remember the sales person asking me, "If I meet all your expectations tonight, is there any reason why you won't drive this car home tonight?" What a fantastic question.

You can mimic this with a client by saying something like, "If I meet all your expectations today, is there any reason why I may not be the Project Manager for this project?" Or, "If I meet all your expectations today, is there any reason why I may I won't get this contract?" You will certainly get a pretty standard reply, such as, "Well, we have to meet with some other candidates". Or, "I have to have my manager approve the budget". But that's quite all right. You have now set the stage.

Continue with the meeting in a normal fashion. When the meeting concludes, shake the client's hand firmly, and casually ask, "So, when can we do this?" Be casual, and keep it very vague and abstract. Do not corner the client in an uncomfortable position.

You have now formed a logical circle.

Going back to the first prep question, in the client's mind, if you have met with all the expectations, you will get a very positive response. More likely then not, you will get a firm date.

If you are met with a common resistance, be positive and state, "Good, I do not see a problem with that. Just remember that..." Restate some of your selling points at this time. If possible, do some homework on your possible competition. Extreme Project Managers shatter their competition, before they even get to the client. You are demonstrating that you certainly are a superior choice, and as far as you are concerned you have the contract. It is just a matter of mere formalities.

CHAPTER THREE

▼

EXTREME MEETINGS

I eat my bagel as I sit through an early meeting at 8:00 AM to form a quick strategy for the 9:00 AM Corporate Communications meeting. Soon after the 9:00 AM, after a quick coffee break, my meeting-packed day leads me to the 10:30 AM meeting, to discuss documentation. At 11:30 AM, I finally get a chance to catch up on my E-mails, and then off I go to a very hectic lunch on the road, to reach a 1:00 PM off site meeting, to discuss Store Security strategies.

While sitting in the meeting, which is running half an hour over, I am already thinking of my 3:00 PM meeting, back at the client site, to assist in knowledge transfer, due to some departing consultants. All this, and I was not even the Project Manager...I was just assisting a very competent PM. At the rates the PM's get today, it is every manager's responsibility to reduce the time spent in meetings, and to optimize every moment spent around the conference table.

But meetings are a fact of life for a manager, especially a Project Manager. Clearly, the management methodology has not evolved to a point where meetings can be executed to its maximum efficiency and effectiveness. Hence, comes a solution from Extreme PM...Extreme Meeting. Extreme Meeting accomplishes two main objectives. It uses the project staff in an efficient manner for better productivity, and it reframes the Project Manager's time and importance.

Side Alpha Side Bravo

Two heads are better then one. How many times have you heard this cliché? Now let me ask you, how many times have you used this to your advantage? Side Alpha–Side Bravo or SASB (pronounced sas-bee), is extremely useful for generating new ideas or solutions. It involves breaking up the team in two sides, and keeping them apart, during brainstorming sessions.

SASB essentially illustrates that the number of solutions generated by *each* side (Side Alpha [SA] or Side Bravo [SB]), will be more then half of the number of solutions generated in a typical (normal) session. In other words, $SA > \frac{1}{2}$ Normal, or $SA + SB >$ Normal; hence, if Normal = 20, then SA and SB will approximately be 15 each. Or, $15 + 15 > 20$, further, $30 > 20$.

The idea here is to use the combined action of the staff to produce results that are more then the project stakeholders usually expect. Solutions generated are given a lot of importance here, because solutions are really a metaphor for a lot of discussions and goals that we endeavor for. And the numbers used in this simple example can easily be 150, instead of 15, and 200, instead of 20. For example, in a project, a few years ago, the original business requirements were not successfully transferred over to the technical requirements. Hence, there was a huge disconnect between what the business side (project sponsor) was expecting, and what the final product provided.

When the business side refused to accept the product, the technical side responded by holding brainstorming sessions, to come up with solutions. The result was a list of a few items that needed to be mitigated. Unfortunately, even after all this effort, there was a vast fissure between the business requirements and the technical requirements.

This is a classic example, where SASB can be implemented. For example, the business side and the technical side can be broken into SA and SB, where half of SA will consist of business and the other half of technical staff. Ditto for the SB side. The resulting proposed solutions can be labeled as 'gaps', and the project can move forward successfully.

Time/Importance Framing

Time/Importance Framing (TIF) occurs, when the opposing party views the subject with a TIF level, which is slightly higher then the normal TIF. A TIF level is basically a point of reference that we use to judge the importance we give to people, right before acting in favor of, or against that person. For example, if a co-worker asks you to attend a meeting, you will go through a thought process, containing of several different criteria that you will use to decide on the action. We always tend to give importance to things in our own priorities, which may, or may not, be beneficial for the project. TIF simply balances those priorities.

If you think that the co-working requesting the meeting has enough value to offer you, you will probably accept the meeting. And depending on how much you value the co-worker's TIF, you will decide on other factors as well. For example, how long are you willing to sit in the meeting? How prone are you to cancel the meeting? And so on. It is very important to understand this concept, as not only your staff, but also everyone else around you is constantly using TIF.

Here is another very interesting way of looking at it. We are changing the *Perceptive Reality* of these people. I introduced a fascinating theory on *Perceptive Reality* last year in my book, "The Eternal Optimist". It will be beneficial to give it a cursory glance. Here is an excerpt from it, "People tend to move toward the reality that makes them happy...I have introduced, in the Eternal Optimist, my theory of the *Realm of Perceptive Reality* (RPR). RPR has been whirling around in my mind for some years now; finally I have the chance to articulate it.

*It is based on the very correct premise that there is one, **and only one**, true reality that exists in the universe. And in its most fundamental form, RPR is* *that perception of reality, which we gather and exist in, from* ***that*** *one true reality.* "

CAUTION: It must be understood that TIF is not there to create a phony pompously ostentatious image for the Project Manager. This section is written for experienced Project Managers, who have overcome all the pretentious complexes. *And as this is Extreme Meetings, form the Extreme Project Management series, some of the ideas maybe—well—extreme.* But remember that in a nutshell, we are changing the perceptive reality of these people, and are helping them put our time and importance in the right frame, to produce the most efficient results for the project stakeholders. Following are some of the components of TIF:

The Departure

For your staff to form a positive TIF level, you must demonstrate that your time is valuable, and that you are important. Choose a routine meeting, such as a recurrent Status Meeting, so all the regular staff members are present. Around ten minutes or so in the meeting (to ensure everyone is present), announce in a nonchalant way that you have to leave early for another meeting. Do not explain with whom, for what, or give any details. Give the appearance that you have places to go; people to see, who are apparently at a higher level in the pecking order.

The Invitees

When you schedule a meeting, limit your invitees, unless it is a brain-storming, or solutions planning session. The less the attendees, the less time it will take to conduct the meeting. This also gives the impression that the people invited have a particular status in the project. This is particularly true for Status Meetings, especially if you have it several times a week. Only team leads and project managers (in case you are fortunate enough to be running a mammoth project with multiple projects tying in) should be invited to status meetings.

Verbiage and Body Language

Verbiage and body language are great methods to control the length of the meeting. If you are the manager, you already know that you must lean forward, if you want to show interest and encourage the person speaking in the meeting. The opposite is also true. If you want to cut down a lengthy explanation of a staff member, look at your watch, lean back, or just turn your head away from the speaker. This will break the speaker's pattern, and will give you a chance to interject, without seeming rude or uninterested.

Carefully choose your words, if you have an enthusiastic group of people pitching ideas at you (which inadvertently turns into its own lengthy discussions). You certainly do not want to discourage a passionate group; at the same time you do not want a meeting going on indefinitely. For example, if you are in a feverish brainstorming session, by saying, "what else?" in a slightly loud and in a somewhat eager manner after every idea, you will certainly ensure that even more ideas will be launched at you. However, just say in a muted tone, "is there anything else?" after an offered idea, and you will almost guarantee an immediate transformation of your group members to a virtually non-participant crowd.

Liquid

Recently, after consuming mass quantities of black coffee, I found myself in a meeting, sitting at the far end of a very crowded conference room, away from the door. Fifteen minutes in the meeting, I had this overwhelming desire to bolt for the door, and to the rest room in the next hallway. But it was an important meeting, with important people. As I sat there, cross-legged and suffering, I realized the power of liquid!

This method is great for problem meetings that persistently run over its allocated time. If you want to keep a meeting short, keep plenty of coffee, tea, water, juices, and anything that flows and tastes good. Be a good host and set an example by keeping a clear glass or mug (so the participants can see that you have your container full). Don't forget to keep sipping from it constantly. Majority of the staff will follow your actions. Within 30 to 45 minutes, I guarantee the staff members to get edgy and sub-consciously trying to end the meeting. This all may sound comical, but it is a great way to manage TIF.

Always remember to keep your TIF in check. Have a constant vigil for anything that threatens it. Extreme Meeting is particularly designed for combating lower TIF. But do not forget the big picture, TIF is designed to generate efficient results for the project, by managing the meetings more proficiently.

Conference Disclosure

One very important technique I learned is a combination of using conference calling, to save time in commute, and having more then one meeting at a time. It is true; there is no substitution of having a face-to-face meeting. However, when there is a time crunch, one must use every weapon available.

If you work in a large corporate center, you may be wasting many valuable minutes just going from room to room for several different meetings. One of my client's had their headquarters on many acres of land. Their office complex was spread out within this compound. When they started their new web page project, the team was allocated office spaces all throughout this gigantic infrastructure, The team members, especially the consultants, were literally spread out all over the complex, including the two extreme ends of the massive structure.

It was a task just to walk from one office to the other. I had to dodge the lunch crowd by the cafeteria in the middle of the complex, the long lines at the reception area at the front of the complex, and endure the lonely ten-minute walk at the end of the newly constructed, and quite isolated wing. Not to mention the many dollars I spent on lattes, passing the coffee shop.

A good strategy would have been just to have conference calls, instead of taking the long walks to the offices. Sometimes that means to do a bit more coordination, and spend a little time and effort on planning up front. For example, little groups of two or three members may have to be invited to conference rooms or cubicles closest to them. But this front-loading of time and effort is worth it, as the time saved is not only yours, but all the team members involved.

Conference calls, especially if you call the meeting, instead of every-body piling in one room is also handy, when you want to maneuver several different meetings in one. For example, if your team is working on several different functionalities of the application, with several different team leads in charge of each of the functionality, you can spend a lot of time in status meetings, if you break the meetings down to individual basis. It is much easier (*psychologically and physically*) to call a meeting, and have the team leads call in the conference lines. Let me clarify and qualify that statement.

Lets say that you are a team lead on a large project called Financial Systems. Your part of the project is called Payment Portals. There are two other parts of the project, Loan Rules and Security Procedures, which have little to do with your job and duties. If you receive a meeting request from your Project Manager for a meeting to discuss Financial Systems, your first response will be, "Do I have to be there? I have tons of things to do".

You may not articulate, but surely your response will be similar.

By sending individual meeting requests to team members, *which relates to their particular theme*, you cut down any acrimonious feelings your meetings may generate. For example, as a team lead, you may get a phone-meeting request to discuss issues relating to Payment Portals. Of course, proper maintenance is required to any Extreme Project Management methodology that you may use. For example, in this case, you must always be the first on the line, in the conference call, and you must regulate the meeting very skillfully, as not to make the meeting very specific to any one topic.

Layered Agenda

Layered Agenda becomes crucial, when the projects are strapped for time. Well, all projects are strapped for time, but I mean those that are *especially* strapped for time. Ensure that you have prepared an official agenda. Just knowing that the meeting will not ramble on for eternity will put a lot of people at ease. The Layered Agenda puts another dimension in your ability to control the meeting.

The Layered Agenda is like an onion. It has an outer layer, which you will expose to the attendees, and you will be in complete control on how many layers you want to peel off. Think of it as an outline for a book, with a list of chapters. These chapters will be the only aspect of the Layer Agenda uncovered to others. The inside layers are like the topics within those chapters, and depending on the time, and how deep you want to dig in a particular topic, and with whom, you will select those subsequent layers. For example, in a meeting on the Financial Systems project:

Below is a good visual for how the Layered Agenda can work, but as far as agendas go, as discussed earlier, it is even more effective to put it in an outline form.

- ✓ Payment Portals
    - ◯ Storefront access
    - ◯ Online Access
        - ■ Web Interface
            - ◆ Online Security
            - ◆ Online Profiles
- ✓ Loan Rules
    - ◯ Credit Profiles
        - ■ Fed Rules

- ■ International Laws
  - ◆ Overseas Security
- ✓ Security Procedures
  - ○ General Security
  - ○ Online Security (include Jack from Payment in discussions)
  - ○ Security laws (include John from Loans in discussions)

Ad Hoc

Regularly scheduled meetings are great for certain things. For example, weekly, or even daily, status meetings are common all over the corporate world. In fact, I am a huge believer in Status meetings. But too many of them, and you have an unacceptable number of downtime. I have been in many meetings, where people actually run out of things to say, and are forced to babble. Or the team just drift off to other unrelated subjects, like discussing today's mortgage rates, or how Tim from Project X is not going to make his deadline.

So, what is the answer? Certainly status meetings are required. I think a compromise is the best solution. First, pick the number of status meetings (or any kind that you are compelled to have), and divide it at least in half. Then use the Ad Hoc technique. For example, if you like status meetings on Mondays, Wednesdays, and Fridays, schedule it for Mondays only. Then whenever you feel like discussing a particular topic, or have the team be aware of the collective status, just swiftly round up the team leads, and quickly go over your agenda. At the least, this gives you the option of manipulating the time and frequency of the meetings.

Surely, there are other more known good measures for having a productive meeting session, such as having an agenda (if only for yourself), making phone and room arrangements in advance, and following up with the team members. By combining the creative techniques of Extreme Project Management, using best practices, and keeping the client's need in sight, you can have some dynamic and very productive meetings.

▼

CHAPTER FOUR

EXPECTATION ESCALATION

Expectation Escalation is reaching a state, where a specified amount of work is completed to a superior quality in general, than its preceding state, as a result of an optimistic objective.

This state is principally dominant in the project staff. A Project Manager comes to the final estimates as a result of the input from many different sources. Any one member or group of the project staff will not have the complete picture, to ascertain the exact timeframe of a distinct component of the project.

Pretense Irony

A concept called Pretense Irony comes into play here. Pretense Irony is defined as:

"A circumstance, where one's superior knowledge and experience allows the person to make a declaration, which may or may not reflect the actual reality and fact of that particular timeline, at the same time making a better decision, which is beneficial for the client, and other interested parties, as well as fending off the competition, due to a more competitive forecast."

"Before Timeline" represents the timeline-forecast state of the project before the start of the project, and the "After Timeline" represents the actual state of the project, after completion.

Thus, if you take the Pretense Irony in account in the equation, it stands to reason that the staff will not complete the project in time. However, as the goals of the timeline were somewhat embellished, the staff will not meet the goals, *but still achieve a higher goal then normal*, as the natural effort of the staff will be to meet the stated goal.

Another derivative of Expectation Escalation is the fact that you (the management) will discern their results as a success, even though the project staff did not meet the exact objectives. The staff will appreciate that their genuine efforts were rewarded, and not just the "bottom line". What is the big picture here? You have just created a more satisfied and indebted employees for your client. You have acquired another win-win notch for your and your company's professional belt.

Status Report

In order to attain the larger picture of Expectation Escalation, several techniques must be in place to drive the workers to that particular goal. One of the goals of the EPM is to use the current best practices of the Project Management environment, and incorporate or enhance those practices to reach EPM goals.

Status reports are a great way of escalating the expectations, by declaring to the employees what achievements you expect from them every week. For this to be effective, the proper status reports are desired.

It seems as if complexity in a project is inversely proportional to status reports. As things get complicated in the workplace, both in methodology and technology, status reports get simpler. Either the Project Managers, or the team leads, do not want to be bothered with the avalanche of information, or just do not understand the content. Either way, it is okay. As the Project Manager, one does not have to study every molecule of information.

By giving the impression that information is not necessarily needed in the status reports, a manager erroneously sends out the signal that the information is not significant. Nothing could be farther from the truth. Even if the manager does not fully understand the material, it is important to have that information, more so for the person making the report, then the Project Manager.

It would be beneficial to take a closer look at status reports. Consider the average status report prepared by a team lead on a typical project. It includes the following information:

From: John Leader
To: Jack Manager
Date: Ending December 10, 2001

Work in Progress:
Assigned work to the programmers for the password character constrains
Attend morning status meetings.

Work Planned:
Update project plans for additional modules
Continue attending meetings

Comments:
Days off for end of month

An alternative status report can demand more robust information, forcibly throwing the report maker in the midst of the subjects being discussed, as well as giving the team member a little more feeling of substance. The report can also be shared between team members to generate a more hearty understanding of the subject and the crux of the project.

Here is an alternate report:

From: John Leader
To: Jack Manager
Date: Ending December 10, 2001

Describe Accomplishments this Week:

Describe any Concerns or Issues:

Describe plans for Next Week:

Message for the Team:
Attachments to Support this Report:

By proclaiming the team lead's work as "accomplishments", you are accreting a positive psychological image on the work done this week by the team members. Other attributes, such as providing more space for the team member to put the thoughts down and giving the status report the look and feel of a "report", will help your cause as well.

Invite the employee to share any concerns, comments, or issues freely. Although, ensure that they know to use some common sense, and bring concerns, which may be deemed politically incorrect in our complex world, to your private attention.

This status report also hints, under the "Message for the Team" section, that all the team members will share the report. This encourages the report writer to not only voice special concerns, but to distribute any other information that may be helpful to the other team leads in completing the project. The sharing of information will open trust barriers, and expedite status meetings, as basic information has already been introduced in the status report.

Finally, this kind of report clearly offers to accept any attachments to go along with the accomplishments of the week. As a matter of fact, it should be made clear to the team leads, to make sure and include any information, such as special coding done my programmers, new tables created by the database team, unique principles developed by the economics team, particular blueprints shaped by the architectures, or any other pertinent information to be attached for the benefit of enlightenment and encouragement for the whole team.

Goal Setting

Equally important to the team's long-term expectations are the goals that are set, or the goals that are perceived to be set. The goal setting that goes on in the work environment is quite different then the goal setting in our personal lives. The difference is that when we first imagine something in the future that we may acquire, it excites us. Everything in our thoughts, our actions, our attitudes, and our complete outlook, adjusts and adapts to acquire that particular acquisition. However, at work, in a particular project, there is no excitement for the hunt.

There are really no acquisitions, just timelines on the project plan.

Our goal then is just to complete those tasks, which are necessary to complete the project. Unfortunately, there is a connection between goals, expectations, and performance. And with such powerless goals, there is a definite lack of lofty expectations. Hence, no goals are set high enough to push the team members to perform to their limits.

The EPM can assess the employee to see how far this person can reach, based on the past results and the present attitude. A goal is then set, which is considerably higher then the person is expected to reach. This is where we tie in Expectation Escalation. Take a look at the definition again and tie it to elevated goals.

Expectation Escalation is reaching a state, where a specified amount of work is completed to a superior quality in general, than its preceding state, as a result of an optimistic objective.

This can be quite controversial in some occasions. I have identified at least two instances, where you may have trouble. The first is where the person being worked on may be too scared to continue, due to the fear of failing. This is easily overcome by some cautious sensibility toward the employee. It must be clearly stated that the expectations stand, due to budget contains, short development schedule, or whatever is appropriate for the project. But it is also very important to put the person at ease, explaining that the consequences of not meeting the expectations are not that dire.

The next scenario of resistance is quite difficult to overcome. This is when someone other then the employee interferes with Expectation Escalation. Usually it is with the best of intentions. The best example I can give you to put this in perspective is when I was in the wonderful city of Atlanta, in the winter of 1999. I was enjoying a gig in the Atlanta city hall, which made the weekends available to me to do what I pleased. I decided to volunteer for a program, which prepared high school kids for the SAT exam.

The group of kids I was working with scored around 600 in their practice exams. If you have been exposed to SAT's, you will know that this is not nearly enough to acquire admission in any good college. My strategy was to set a goal of 1300 for the kids to reach by summer. Based on my theory of Expectation Escalation, I was sure that they would score at least 1100, and will have a shot at a good state school.

Well, there was a whiz kid of about sixteen the organization was using as a consultant, because he apparently had scored the highest in the state of Georgia in the SAT exam. When he heard about my theory in the training period for the teachers, he protested that we would only be setting the kids up for failure. Now I ask you, whom would you listen to? A kid who just scored almost a perfect score out of a possible 1600, or someone like me, who barely broke 1200?

Regardless of the result of that particular situation (the kid won), it is important to remember that sometimes you have to be a little crafty on how you apply the Extreme Project Management principals. Be aware of who has a say in your decisions, and how you can maneuver around it. In this case, if you are using Expectation Escalation, then do your best to confine the matter of discussions between you and the employee.

With practice you will notice that setting superior goals, which at first glance may seem to unattainable, you will send forces in motion, which will astound you. I do not mean to be metaphysical or spiritual, but just to tell you that sometimes we simply underestimate the resolve and the talent of our coworkers and ourselves. "Expect away" and see the wonderful results.

CHAPTER FIVE

▼

RISK EQUALIZER

I have a strong distaste for loose ends; especially, if they were created and maintained outside of my immediate control. So when I started coming across risks, which predated my arrival at a project, I became somewhat angst-ridden. I have full confidence in my work; however, when it comes to inheriting years of assumptions, without any particular accountability, or foreseeable resolution, I am prone to take some kind of an action. Hence, I created the Risk Equalizer.

"Risk Equalizer is an action point that challenges risks defined by the project, and converts them to assumptions, by assigning each pre-defined risk a responsibility, then assigning new risks, with improved net effect. "

It is normal for a few risks to be left over. Prior to the creation of the Project Plan, even previous to the formation of the Project Charter, a cursory glance at the risks is essential. The next step is to conduct a meticulous risk analysis, and allot new risks. The end result of Risk Equalization is that you are left with fewer risks that were beyond your control, and are now confronting risks that have been defined by you, creating a more controllable net effect for your attentiveness.

A word of caution here...Before performing Risk Equalization, carefully study the client's version of the risk analysis. For risks allotted a rating of 'high' or 'critical'. Be very cautious in converting to assumptions. There are two primary reasons for this, Discounting Risk and Receiving Risk.

Discounting Risk

The fist reason is the sensitivity of the client. If the client has designated a risk to he 'high' or 'critical', it may seem as careless (although an Extreme PM is never careless) in your part to 'discount' the risk.

There is a mistaken identity for the Project Managers, especially consulting Project Managers. It is well imagined in countless client circles that Project Managers make $1000 an hour and work four hours a day. Although I drool at such prospects, obviously it not true. Hence, unfortunately as it may seem, there lies the proverbial chips on the shoulders of some of the employees at the client site.

So when you discount a risk, you are essentially challenging the client. You are indirectly indicating that your risk analysis is better then theirs. At the same time, the Project Managers are seen as outside the circle of workers. The core circle workers being the people who report to you, and see you as basically the one who makes the task lists, and attends meetings. Hence, as you are seen outside of the circle, you may be wrongly accused of not "caring" enough for the project, and you may be blamed for discounting the risk for personal gains. That is, either to speed up the project, or simply to divert attention from a difficult issue.

A good remedy is to observe carefully the sensitivity of the risk to the client and the project team, and do not immediately touch those risks that may seem like "untouchables". In fact, it may be wise to have a secret list of Touchable and Untouchable risks. When you are dealing with Untouchable risks, the equalization may seem logical, but may not be politically prudent.

Touchable Risk Examples:

Unknown number of workstations required

Delivery of software not set

Training schedule for users is not set

Rules validation from the federal government not received

Confidentiality of records may be compromised with the present code

Untouchable Risk Examples:

Risk mitigation status inaccurate

The vendors chosen have a bad track record

The skill levels of the programmers may be in question

The expansion schedule for the project is not planned

Receiving Risk

The second reason is the conversation of risk to assumption. As a responsibility must be assigned to each assumption, the 'receiving' party may consider it too perilous, both politically and professionally.

I am not aware of any existing organization that does not suffer from political afflictions. Assigning risks for the purpose of conversion is precarious, at best. You will be treading uncertain territory, if you are at a client site. If you are indigenous to the organization, then prepare to make enemies. A risk is like a hot potato. No one wants to hold it.

One remedy to this situation may to test out the receiving parties. Once you have identified a Touchable risk, assign it to the person most logical to receive it. Wait a few days for the reaction. If you receive none, consider yourself fortunate and move on to the next Touchable risk. If you receive a lot of opposition to the conversion, simply identify your next target for the conversion assignment, and hand over the risk to that person.

If you follow this remedy, you must proceed cautiously and be able to smoothly take off the assigned risk from the hands of the previous assignee and hand it off to the next recipient. Eventually, you will have to decide, if you keep running out of recipients, whether you want to convert the Touchable risk to Untouchable.

Risk Equalizer is a modern tool to serve the client better. It battles scope creep and creates a win-win situation for the client, or the project owner. And as with all innovative ideas, they may be deemed a bit divisive or even be uncomfortable to use for a Project Manger, without the proper people skills. Remember, the primary decree here is not just to make the numbers look good, but also to serve the client, efficiently and effectively.

CHAPTER SIX

EXTREME EFFORT ANALYSIS AND METHODOLOGY

▼

Before you start any project, you will almost certainly be asked to come up with some kind of an estimate. Fortunately, a lot of time, the Request for Proposal (RFP) has already addressed this issue, and a detailed estimate relating to effort has been provided to the client, or the project sponsor. However, chances are that the immediate person you are dealing with has not read the response to the RFP. Hence, an Extreme Project Manager is always prepared to present a customized effort analysis and methodology.

The reason behind this is not to be redundant, or provide some kind of a back up, but to customize the analysis, for your advantage. The idea is to be a little more wide-ranging and general. Break up the analysis into two main categories: Value and Cursory Phases.

Value

An Extreme Project Manager never misses an opportunity to express some hints, if there are any elements of added value. Start the analysis with bulleted statements, which emphasizes value. For Example, for a recent Program Structure project for a small company in Texas, I added the following values, before I started the analysis:

✓   Ability for the Program Office to centralize the information

✓   Opportunity to sell the new program infrastructure to outside customers

✓   Showcase the structured program office as a proven deliverable to clients

✓   Improved presentation of the company to outside vendors and potential venture capitalists

It is important to notice that these values were never mentioned in the response to RFP. When you start the analysis with value statements, which may seem to be 'extras', the work that you do will be magnified, and any resistance to your estimates will be dissolved.

Cursory Phase

Break up the analysis in three phases. Preparation Phase, Principal Effort, and Termination and Preservation Phase. I have seen some managers feel the need to detail out the phases. I recommend against it. Try to stay at a high level; you do not want any conflicts with the original response to RFP.

Preparation phase

The first phase is always the Preparation phase. In this phase the effort and time used for research, forecasting, and laying out the foundation is identified. Once again, statements are made, which identifies the functions for each phase. For example:

Preparation Phase—Eight employees—Four Weeks (8 x 40 x 4 = 1280 hours)

1—Detail analysis of requirements gathered from management interviews

2—Plan the different modules required for infrastructure study

3—Study of the different Automated Management Systems available in the market

4—Design architecture for development

Principal Effort phase

The second phase the Principal Effort phase. This phase consists of the bulk of the work, as far as the effort hours are concerned, but not necessary the time. For example, you may have eight people involved in the Preparation phase, for four weeks. In the Principal Effort phase you may have forty people working for three weeks, developing and documenting, what has been prophesied for them in the Preparation phase. Of course, depending on the complexity of the project, the second phase may be measured in years. But my point is that it takes a lot more man-hours to complete this phase. For Example:

Principal Effort Phase—Forty employees—Fifty-two weeks (40 x 40 x 52 = 83,200 hours)
1—Develop a working model
2—Test the product

Project Termination and Preservation
phase

The third phase, which is also the smallest, is the Project Termination and Preservation phase. This is quite an unusual name, as termination and preservation are actually antonyms. The purpose of this phase is not just knowledge transfer and project closeout, but a continued maintenance of the project. This phase may contain:

> Project Termination and Preservation Phase—Four Employees—Four Weeks (4 x 40 x 4 = 640 hours)
> 1—Write documentation for the product or the process
> 2—Develop training material

Hence the objective of this methodology is to accentuate the positive values generated by the effort, as well as give a good indication of the time it would take in labor hours to complete the project. If you develop comprehensive training programs and good documentation, it will also provide the client an additional incentive to approach you for phase two of the project, or any future programs.

CHAPTER SEVEN

─────────▼─────────

THE HOUSE OF DEFECTS

As a Project Manager, planning is the most crucial part of the project. However, planning does not end, when the product is fully coded, even if the QA is scheduled for a completely different department. When the application finally goes into production, the Project Manager must be held answerable, if something major goes awry. And there is good reason for it. According to the Gartner Institute, if an application goes down in an unplanned fashion, the company looses $100,000 an hour.

The Extreme Project Management principal dictates that Project Managers conduct their own QA, before it is passed on to production. This is not the same QA, as performed by the QA department; the Project Manager's process resides at a higher level in the big picture, specifically to track the defects, at a minimum, before it leaves the Project Manager's capable hands.

The Process

Any good Defect Tracking program starts by planning the process. For this purpose, it is best to stay at a high level. A typical process that I have used in the past is the TDT (Trifold Defect Tracking) process. The reason it is called Trifold Defect Tracking is because if you put the process flow down on paper, and fold the paper in three places, the process is broken down in three clean sections.

Origin

Section one is the Origin. In this section, the tester discovers the defect and logs it in a pre-existing (discussed later) form, then forwards the defect form to the individual team lead for that particular build. It is important to remember that there must be only one contact for each build or module. It is the responsibilities of the team leads to further disseminate the information. This ensures better control and adequate communication in the project.

Having said that let me add that it is also useful to have a contact person for the business side, if the project you are working on leans toward business functionality. This person only represents the business, and has nothing to do with the assigning of the defects to the appropriate team leads.

The business contact is especially important in QA status meetings, where the previous days defects (discovered by the QA team) are identified, and assigned to the team leads, to be fixed. Having the business contact present, either in person or via phone, helps in identifying those defects that do not exactly belong in the defect category. The business contact, in this case, can help interpret the original project requirements.

As an EPM, you may have to operate at a slightly more complex level then a traditional Project Manager. At this point of the defect-tacking model, you have to act as the gatekeeper. You must analyze and scrutinize each proposed defect to ensure that they are actually defects, and not just a misinterpretation of the requirements. At times you have to play the detective, the lawyer, and the judge to argue your case. It goes without saying that you must know the business and technical requirements well.

Leader Decision

Section two is the Leader Decision. In this section, the team lead, decides what priority to give this particular defect. This is done in conjunction with the business side. This section is also known as the 'Political' section. It may be painfully obvious to the IT team lead what the priority of the defect fix should be; nevertheless, the business side has to be consulted. Low priority items, such as cosmetic issues, can be sent to a pending area, while high priority items, such as code defects can be routed through the process.

The level of involvement of the business side is usually determined by the amount of stake it has in the project. If the project is primary a module of a company, such as a Financial Systems project, the business side will probably be a major player. The team leads, in this case would have to be advised to use extreme political prudence. For example, the ability of the user to check the latest interest rates may not sound like much to a technical person, and the defect may be routed to a low priority area. However, to a businessperson, the technical issue may be irrelevant, and the defect may appear to be a critical issue.

This may cause a potential problem, in project that is time constrained. The QA department and the upper management are typically pressing the project manager, to railroad the defects through the process, as soon as possible. A potential solution to combat the business side then may be to hold the defects as a Business Issue.

A Business Issue falls somewhere in the gray area, which does not have to be immediately addressed, as it is somewhat contended whether the defect in question was even supposed be part of the project. Some Business Issues are later converted to Change Control, so that particular feature may be included in the project. Business Issues and Change Control will be covered in detail later.

Assign and Fix

The third section is the Assign and Fix section. This section is the simplest of all, but the most time consuming. The team lead assigns the defect to a developer to be fixed. Although, this is a 'defect tracking' process, the fix must be completed, before TDT process can be declared finished, as the goal is to have the application ready to go to the QA department, not just to 'know' what the defects are. There will be many QA processes that the Project Manager may not have the resources for, like Load Testing, which are traditionally done in the QA department. But an Extreme Project Manager makes it a priority for the product to be in 'as perfect as can be' shape, before it is presented to anybody outside of the project.

During the Assign and Fix section, you may have to allocate some more resources at the beginning of the QA stage, as you will experience a surge in defects initially. It is actually a double whammy, because the first few defects found by the QA will be labeled of a critical nature, and your team will experience some jostle in completing the fix.

Documents

The TDT process only takes a few pieces of documents to complete. As always, I will insist that a professional Technical Writer is used to create forms and other documents. The two typical documents are the TDT form and the TDT database.

The TDT form is a simple form created in Word. It is made available to every tester on the team, or the QA department personnel. The tester merely fills out the form, which consists of fields, such as Defect Number, Defect Description, Module or Build, Date Opened, Priority, Date Closed, and Tester Name. The database is an uncomplicated Access database, which mirrors the Word form exactly. For example, each of the field in the Word form corresponds to the field on the

Another step the EPM takes to ensure a complete control of the project is to assign a different number to the defects that flow in from the QA. The project will maintain two separate TDT forms, one for the QA to fill out, and one for the team to handle the fix. For example, when the defect comes down from the QA, it may have a defect number of PAYMENT PORTAL 101. As the defects gets handed down to the programmers on your team, who will apply the fix, it may have a defect number of PP001.

Once the fix is applied, the defect number gets converted to PAY-MENT PORTAL 101, and the fix is passed on to QA to test again. Only you and the person in charge of the TDT process may have the key to the defect numbers. This stops both, the business and the QA department, from interfering too much in your project. A simple form may be used to keep track of the defect number conversions.

Lab

Before the TDT process begins, ensure that the testing environment does not have a huge disconnect with the true production environment. It is not expected for the IT Project Manager to have access to all the bells and whistles of a QA department's lab, but some reasonable reality reproduction is expected.

For example, a few years ago, I was at a major Fortune 500 company, working on a state-of-the-art product, used in emergency vehicles. The core usability existed while the vehicle was in motion, possibility at high speeds. However, the lab environment consisted of a few prototypes connected with all kinds of different off the shelf cables. This is the kind of disconnect I am referring to.

Even if the project is not that technical, it is useful to have a functional lab. For example, the product you are working on may eventually have 30,000 users. You will need to have the right resources to simulate that kind of a load on the system. Not just in technical term, but in human terms as well, such as adequate personnel for a call center.

Finally, it is certainly the responsibility of the Extreme Project Manager to ensure that all the components come together at some level. The TDT process works best, when it is in sync with the rest of the QA mechanisms, whether it is at the development, under complete control of the Project Manager, or at the production level.

Chapter Eight

———————▼———————

Breakthrough Review

Perspectives

One of the problems faced by managers, when reviewing employee performance is the fairness and objectivity of the review. I strongly believe that the employer should be able to decide and set its own standards for the review, even if it appears 'too harsh' or 'too high' to the general public, as long as it is ethical and reasonable.

I see a different problem though. I see the problem from the perspective of the employee, being reviewed. The reason is that often we forget the big picture, that is, the good of the company. If the employee feels threatened or unfairly judged, the employee 's performance will suffer, and the company's performance will suffer. It all boils down to one thing, the employee must be happy. This is particularly true if the manager is a consultant, with a staff primarily made up of client employees.

RABOHA

The answer to this problem is to review the employee in the employee's environment. The answer is called RABOHA (Review and Appraisal Based on Human Attributes). The manager must observe the employee, then act upon that observation by giving certain advice to the employee, or take action to change the environment. Here is the story of RABOHA, followed by a comprehensive interactive review process.

Several years ago, when I was involved with a project in a desert town in West Texas, I had the opportunity to get to know a few of my employees outside of the work environment. I was able to conduct a study, which five years later ultimately gave birth to RABOHA. I recognize that my method was quite intuitive and somewhat unempirical, but I wish to share the chain of events, so you may have certain imminence behind the motivation of RABOHA.

I had noticed that although the employees had a certain professional disposition at work, they fundamentally kept the same emotional character throughout the day. For example, if employee X was typically happy during the off work hours, then he was frequently happy during the work hours. And if employee Y was mostly irritable and grumpy during the off work hours, then she generally irritable and grumpy during the work hours.

At this stage, I was reflecting on two abstractions:

✓ *Just because they appear to be happy, didn't necessarily mean that they were happy.*
✓ *If they were happy, did they work better?*

Hence, I was trying to get a handle on some basic attributes of human emotions, and its subsequent effects and possible manipulation of those attributes for better production.

Well, from informal observations, and years of experience, I can unequivocally tell you that a happy worker is the best worker. Having established that rationale, the next reasonable phase was to determine when the workers were happy. Hence, I developed HES (Human Emotive Scale). HES was simply a scale of 0 to 10. The subjects had to mark on the scale every half-hour, recording their emotional status; 0 being extreme depression, and 10 being tremendously happy. To my surprise, out of the ten employees I had picked, all of them were around 3 or 4, 90% of the time.

After the above experiment, I realized that instead of going in each employee's life and changing them to be 'happy' employees, perhaps I could have a methodology, which will conduct reviews *and* make specific recommendations, to improve the quality of employees and to increase the overall production.

Hence, after 60 more months of gathering data and observing humans in industries like Aviation, Biologics, Finance, Retail, and Education, I came up with RABOHA. RABOHA is a very uncomplicated review process, where a manager can select the attributes relating to a particular employee, then merely going to the corresponding 'action paragraph' and applying that recommendation to the employee. In fact, selecting enough attributes from the worksheet, and matching them with the corresponding 'action paragraph' can form a full Appraisal/Review Report. As always, I will insist that a professional Technical Writer is used to create forms and other documents.

Review Report Worksheet

(Feedback on Positive and Negative Attributes Selected)

Attribute—OFFERS NEW IDEAS:

Yes:

Remarks:

No:

Remarks:

Let the employee see the big picture. Sometimes the employee may see a 'better' or 'quicker' way of doing things. However, in the big picture, with the new idea introduced, all the components may not work together as well. Keep a very open mind, when the employee suggests an idea; that is, consider the possibility of changing a 'certain' way of doing things.

Attribute—FUNCTIONS INDEPENDTLY:

Yes:

Remarks:

No:

Remarks:

The employee must see the team's objectives clearly, so as not to trample on the end results. Very carefully keep tabs on the goals articulated by the employee; it must be directly aligned with that of the company's. Evaluate the employee's given tasks. Ensure that those tasks are met reasonably by the employee, and are not compromised by the employee's independent actions. If the employee's duties are met, then give the employee more responsibility.

Attribute—LACKS INITIATIVE:

Yes:

Remarks:

No:

Remarks:

Let the employee feel free to suggest new ideas and take action on them, as the present way may not be the best fit in the process. The employee actually may possess some unique quality, which can be beneficial to the company. Introduce the employee to key players in the team, so that they may influence the employee. Expose the employee to the customers. When asked for advice, delay in giving one, and let the employee come up with solution.

Attribute—NOT WILLING TO TAKE RISKS:

Yes:

Remarks:

No:

Remarks:

Give the employee an opportunity to work on a small project, where the end result does not constitute a great degree of significance. Let the employee be aware that wrong or inappropriate decisions will be permissible. Stress the company mission, and how certain decisions will have to be made to accomplish these objectives. When a change is noticed in the employee's behavior, make sure proper reward is given; even it is in the form of encouraging words.

Attribute—VERY PRODUCTIVE:

Yes:

Remarks:

No:

Remarks:

The employee must give precedence to the tasks that have priority. That is, the employee has to be productive on the tasks that's summoning for prioritization, in line with the company goals. Reorganize and overhaul the job requirements of the employee, if needed, but ensure that the employee keeps the edge on being productive. At the same time the employee must concentrate on the business that maters most. Do not allow the employee to work in isolation, let the team share in the richness of productivity.

Attribute—USES TIME EFFICIENTLY AND EFFECTIVELY:

Yes:

Remarks:

No:

Remarks:

Reevaluate the employee's schedule carefully. Appraise and estimate the major tasks the employee has completed in the past two to four weeks. You have to ensure that the efficiency that is being modeled is actually work that deserves the time and attention that the employee has been giving it. Give the employee a particularly difficult task, and thoughtfully analyze the time spent on it. This will give you a good idea of the employee's true potential.

Attribute—NOT ORGANIZED:

Yes:

Remarks:

No:

Remarks:

Start from the basics. Have the employee clean the work area of all loose papers and out of date work. Next, ensure that the employee is using all the computer resources in an optimal basis. If the employee is not a high tech employee, train the employee on the operating system of the desktop. Reduce paper by storing and backing up everything that can be stored electronically. Carefully keep track of the employee's *path of productivity* on a daily basis, that is, see in what order the employee accomplishes the tasks on an hour-to-hour basis.

Attribute—PROCRASTINATES:

Yes:

Remarks:

No:

Remarks:

Help the employee prioritize the workday. The employee must spend the first ten minutes of the day making a list of things to be done, arranged in order of importance. Ensure that the employee has a precise deadline for all the tasks. When these deadlines are met, reward the employee. Make the employee aware that an effort is being made to overcome the procrastination.

Attribute—HAS DIFFICULT PRIORITIZING:

Yes:

Remarks:

No:

Remarks:

The employee must work out of a deadline-based system. Keep all the tasks on the list in view at all times, and ensure that the employee does not pick the tasks that are based on interest, or what the employee feels is of particular importance for whatever reason. Help the employee here identify which tasks are applicable to the company goals and objectives. The employee must keep in touch with other members of the team, to constantly remind oneself that the objectives and priorities must be aligned across teams

Attribute—UNDERSTANDS CUSTOMER NEEDS:

Yes:

Remarks:

No:

Remarks:

Use the employee's understanding of the customer needs, to reevaluate the company wide customer service policies. If needed, revise these policies. The employee must be given a leadership role in the group to further expand the understanding to the rest of the employees to serve as a role model to the other members of the group. Develop training classes based on these new finding and assign this employee to play a key role in designing the course.

Attribute—GOOD DISPOSITION TOWARD CUSTOMERS:

Yes:

Remarks:

No:

Remarks:

Use the employee's disposition toward the customer to further enhance the total customer satisfaction package. Identify what motivated the employee and disseminate this intelligence among other employees. Organize training sessions, if possible, to fulfill this objective.

Attribute—PROMPTLY RESPONDS TO CUSTOMERS:

Yes:

Remarks:

No:

Remarks:

Ensure that the employee is pragmatic and honest toward customer expectations. Monitor the employee's zeal to satisfy the customer, and ensure it does not take precedence over the company's ability to provide realistic service. Have recent delivery schedules always available to the employee. Have appropriate rewards ready for the employee for meeting customer needs and for providing exceptional customer service. Grant this employee enough authority to carry out tactical decisions for customer service issues.

Attribute—UNCLEAR ON CUSTOMER NEEDS:

Yes:

Remarks:

No:

Remarks:

Quiz this employee on customer needs and requirements. Keep a tab on the depth of ambiguousness and vagueness this employee displays. Document the level of understanding that the employee has of the current customer needs. Send this employee to training classes to reacquaint with the customer's needs. If all fails, remove this employee from any position that might affect the customer relation adversely.

Attribute—UNRESPONSIVE TO CUSTOMERS:

Yes:

Remarks:

No:

Remarks:

If this customer displays the attribute of being unclear on the customer needs, follow the advice below. However, if the employee is truly unresponsive to customers, only a thorough training on customer satisfaction can solve this problem. As customer service is crucial to any business, have a specific deadline to correct this problem. Be prepared to remove this employee from all customer contacts.

Attribute—UNCLEAR ON CUSTOMER NEEDS:

Yes:

Remarks:

No:

Remarks:

Quiz this employee on customer needs and requirements. Keep a tab on the depth of ambiguousness and vagueness this employee displays. Send this employee to training classes to reacquaint with the customer's needs. If all fails, remove this employee from any position that might affect the customer relation adversely.

Attribute—INTERACTS EFFECTIVELY WITH CO-WORKERS:

Yes:

Remarks:

No:

Remarks:

Let this employee work on many different tasks. Let the employee interact and constantly communicate with other employees. Use this employee as a catalyst to improve communication in the whole organization. Ensure that this employee is clear on company goals, as this employee's vision and value will likely transfer to other employees.

Attribute—PROVIDES ACCURATE REPORTS:

Yes:

Remarks:

No:

Remarks:

Occasionally double check the accuracy of this employee, do not assume that the reports will always be accurate. Besides accuracy, verify that all the important material is included in the reports. If all works out fine, push this employee a little. Assign this employee more work that involves reports. Have this employee report to managers who make significant decisions in the organization.

Attribute—COMMUNICATES WELL:

Yes:

Remarks:

No:

Remarks:

Have this employee attend meetings and other gatherings that include key leaders from the organization and customers. Ensure that this employee has all the proper information and the knowledge to interact in this capacity. Instruct this employee to avert from using too much technical jargon. Train this employee for public speaking and consider expanding the job assignment to include public and customer relations.

Attribute—POOR LISTENER:

Yes:

Remarks:

No:

Remarks:

Observe the employee during a conversation for signs of acknowledgement. If the employee indicates that the information is not being adequately absorbed, ask occasional questions. Ask questions constantly, if a reasonable answer is not given, confront the employee. Help the employee along by assigning books and other training material to improve this improve their listening skills.. Explain to the employee that the job may depend in the employee being more attentive.

Attribute—DOES NOT HAVE A PRESENTABLE APPEARANCE:

Yes:

Remarks:

No:

Remarks:

Determine what makes this employee not have a presentable appearance. Focus on the employee's attitude, demeanor, body language, and clothes. Inform the employee about the company's dress code. If no written policy on dress code exists, provide an example of a co-worker with presentable appearance. Don't single one employee out. Make sure an even standard is observed.

Attribute—UNABLE TO EXPRESS IDEAS:

Yes:

Remarks:

No:

Remarks:

This employee should study the audience, before expressing the ideas. Assist the employee in preparing detailed outlines, for reports and other similar tasks. Offer guidance relating to the use of appropriate rhetoric. Instruct the employee to be as straightforward and direct as possible. Knowledge transfer is important. If this employee continues to have problems with expressing ideas, reassign the employee.

Attribute—WORKS WELL IN A GROUP ENVIRONMENT:

Yes:

Remarks:

No:

Remarks:

Assign this employee a mediator's role during team conflicts. Let the employee communicate candidly with team members. Remind the employee to be impartial and fair in these meetings. Suggest to the team how well they work together, when this employee is present. Encourage other divisions of the organization to apply the employee's skill for their benefit.

Attribute—WORKS TOWARDS COMPANY GOALS:

Yes:

Remarks:

No:

Remarks:

Assign this employee a mediator's role during team conflicts. Ensure that the goals are strategic in nature, as well as tactical. Let the essence of goal setting carry through in the team environment. Scrutinize the goals to ensure that they are distinct and obtainable Periodically review the goals to ensure that they are in-line with the overall goals and vision of the company. Ask for input, when there are organizational changes made that affect the team's previous goals.

Attribute—ABLE TO RESOLVE INTERPERSONAL DISCORD:

Yes:

Remarks:

No:

Remarks:

Have this employee remain objective and unbiased at all times. Examine the motives behind the employee's disposition for the interpersonal skills. Ensure that the ultimate intent and motive for this social grace is not personal in nature. Have the employee mingle and blend in different groups. Allow the employee to play a key role in all meetings and gatherings.

Attribute—FINDS FAULTS IN TEAM MEMBERS:

Yes:

Remarks:

No:

Remarks:

Help the employee understand that the team is working to accomplish the same objectives and goals. Observe the employee for signs of frustration, when dealing with other employees. Examine the background of the employee carefully, to check for any signs of violence in the work environment in the past. If the employee's temperament varies from finding faults to outright verbal criticism, consider sending the employee to sensitivity training.

Attribute—DOES NOT SHARE INFORMATION:

Yes:

Remarks:

No:

Remarks:

After each meeting, interrogate the employee to determine what type of information was disseminated. Inquire whether the employee shared the ideas with every pertinent team member. The notion here is to make the employee perceive and understand that it is mutually advantageous to exchange vital information. Illustrate to the employee the undeviating correlation between the success of the team, and the success of the employee.

Attribute—ADAPTS TO CHANGES:

Yes:

Remarks:

No:

Remarks:

Encourage the employee by elucidating the value of being able to change with the environment. Demonstrate the contribution the employee is making by being able to change. Further encourage the employee to be proactive in the change. Although being adaptive is commendable, ensure that the employee does not just move forward, without any regard to the satisfactory fulfillment of former assignments. Verify that tasks assigned to the employee are fully completed.

Attribute—OPEN TO NEW IDEAS:

Yes:

Remarks:

No:

Remarks:

This employee needs all the support you can give, as long as the ideas are received and ultimately acted upon for the benefit of the organization. Monitor the ideas being fed into this employee to ensure that they are not detrimental to company goals. Help the employee generate new ideas, instead of just acting upon new ideas being furnished.

Assist the employee in being open to all ideas, not just the ones that meet certain employee-defined guidelines.

Attribute—PROACTIVE:

Yes:

Remarks:

No:

Remarks:

Keep track of this employee for at least a few weeks to shadow the effects of the actions taken. Look for scenarios to catch potential problems. Inform the employee to have contingency plans handy, in case of failure of the original plan. Being proactive has its pitfalls; a lot more action items are created, and ultimately acted upon. Assign this employee tasks dealing with customer issues, especially those issues that have suffered from dullness and inaction in the past. Delegate more responsibility to this employee. Quickly promote to bestow more power and authority, so the employee can make the proactive characteristic work more practically and efficiently.

Attribute—DOES NOT ADAPT WITHOUT SUPERVISION:

Yes:

Remarks:

No:

Remarks:

Ask the employee to take ownership of the problem often. Inform the employee that accountability and responsibility will be of significance. Assign the employee substantially difficult tasks, and do not make yourself available that often, for a few weeks. Notice signs of confidence evolving in the employee. Build confidence by conferring with the employee's immediate supervisor to employ similar means of confidence building techniques.

ATTIBUTE—UNWILLING TO TAKE ON VARYING WORK ASSIGNMENT:

Yes:

Remarks:

No:

Remarks:

Inform the employee on the importance of the tasks by giving evidence of the importance of the assignment in the scheme of things. Make the task more engaging to the employee. Probe in to the reason behind the apprehensiveness of the employee to embrace varying work assignments. Structure the task to be a little easier, or respite it down to a manageable size. Acquaint the employee, in a non-threatening manner, with the responsibilities and accountability of his duties. Make evident to the employee how the work assignment will ultimately affect the project.

Attribute—MANAGES FAIRLY:

Yes:

Remarks:

No:

Remarks:

Examine the management style to make sure that it is indeed fair, and just does not appear to be so. At times, when the managers are biased toward the popular employees, the perception can be a little skewed. Have the employee take a management test, if none is available, and then quiz the employee on the issues at stake. Ensure that the employee is very clear on the different issues and their priorities that the team is facing. Give more responsibilities to his team members. Determine the PODC (point of diminishing competency) for this manager, and the group as a whole. See how far this group can be pushed, before evidence of a burn out is experienced. If the employees view this employee as a fair manager, they will undoubtedly have a good PODC.

Attribute—HAS CLARITY IN VISION AND FOCUS:

Yes:

Remarks:

No:

Remarks:

Take this employee's ideas and sculpture it to fit the organization's needs. When the employee suggests an idea, assist the employee in removing bureaucratic obstacles. Refine and clarify the vision to meet company goals and objectives. Seek the employee's input in all significant affairs. Promote this employee in a position, where more strategic initiative is needed.

Attribute—JUDGEMENT IS SOMETIMES BIASED:

Yes:

Remarks:

No:

Remarks:

Study and recognize the reason behind the bias. If it is related to quality, performance, or other legitimate reason, work with the employee to refine the methods. Otherwise clarify the employees role to reflect the seriousness of this shortcoming. Ensure that all your values are in order, as well. Check all the other team members and close associates of this employee to ensure that their judgment and focus is acceptable to company standards.

Attribute—DOES NOT CHALLENGE DIFFICULT ISSUES:

Yes:

Remarks:

No:

Remarks:

Ask the employee to seek the team member's help in making key decisions, with respect to difficult issues, regardless of the complexity. Slowly build the employee's confidence to make the decisions independently. Assign the responsibility of this task clearly to the employee. Stay out of the issue as much as possible. Offer your help to the employee only as a last resort. Once a difficult issue is handled, support the decision attained by the employee.

Attribute—WILLING TO LEARN NEW TECHNOLOGY
AND GAIN KNOWLEDGE:

Yes:

Remarks:

No:

Remarks:

Ensure that the employee is acquiring knowledge, which can be directly
used for the company's benefit... Ask the employee to make a list of skills,
which might need improvement. Make training time available. Draw up a
long-term plan with the employee. Give the training some direction, as to
how it will ultimately benefit the organization. Impress upon the
employee the personal benefits to be gained by advancing oneself in technology and knowledge.

Attribute—CONSCIENTIOUS AND ETHICAL:

Yes:

Remarks:

No:

Remarks:

Assist and encourage this employee in transmitting these qualities to as many employees as possible. Monitor the stability of these merits, and if found to be consistent, move the employee around in different groups and teams. Nourish this belief system even further by rewarding this employee often. Seek this employee's advice, before implementing new policies and procedures. Acquire this employee's assistance in making decisions in issues dealing with ethical problems.

Attribute—HAS TROUBLE WITH TIME MANAGEMENT:

Yes:

Remarks:

No:

Remarks:

Keep a detailed log of every task performed by this employee. Include in the log any deviation from the accepted arrival time in the office. Verify whether the employee is simply taking too much on, or is truly having trouble managing time. In the former case, assist the employee in delegating authority. If needed, secure an assistant for the employee. If the employee is constantly underestimating the time for task completion, investigate the reasons behind it. Ensure that the employee is getting accurate information from the regular sources.

Attribute—GETS INVOLVED WITH OFFICE CHATTER AND GOSSIP:

Yes:

Remarks:

No:

Remarks:

Notice carefully how much time productiveness is being wasted by these undesirable qualities. Observe, but leave the employee alone, if the affect on the company is inconsequential. However, if these habits prove to be a problem, explain to this employee the consequences of being side-tracked and time wastage. Nothing brings the moral down in employees then hearing some worthless and futile gossip. Clarify and control any misinformation already spread. However, be realistic in implementing any plans to remedy this situation.

By reviewing the employee in the employee's environment, the manager can come to a better conclusion, and be very effective in counseling a good course of action, which seems fair to the employee, and be beneficial to the project.

CHAPTER NINE

▼

SITE OF LIFE

Here is something different to breathe life in your project. Have a web site for it. Remember one of the primary objectives is to accentuate your usefulness and worth to the project stakeholders. With a site dedicated to the project, you will be able to show off the accomplishments that you want the company to focus on and illustrate your advanced ideas for managing a project. The Extreme Project Manager (EPM) always shows off at every opportunity.

Image Control and Value

You will use this site mainly for image control. Having your own site for the project will allow you great leverage in divulging information that you wish, in order to create a certain image for your project, and ultimately for yourself. For example, if you meet all your milestones for the week, you can advertise that. At the same time, the site can give you a great platform to sound off any hardships that your project may have suffered. For example, if you missed a major deliverable, you can explain the situation, and thus exonerate yourself.

The site is also a wonderful tool to display the value that you and your team are providing to the company. Just like in the Effort Analysis, this is a good place to display the value added statements. List out the great things the company can do, once the project is completed. Seek out staff members with some great accomplishments or credentials, and list those here, giving the project extra credibility. For example, if you are working on an E-learning project, and you have a PhD in Education on your staff, then publicize that fact. Some of the values that you can accentuate are:

- ✓ Special degrees
- ✓ Past experiences
- ✓ Past achievements in the field
- ✓ Awards
- ✓ Current achievements
- ✓ Project progress

Building with people

The site is great for the morale of your team members. Make sure that you showcase members, who are working on the project, even if their contribution is minimum. Exaggerate their achievements. Everybody has something to offer, and everybody loves to see their name in lights. Make the site available outside of the secured intranet of the company. So the team members can use it to display their work to fresh clients in new projects.

Having said that, keep in mind that you don't want to spend too much time of your resources in building something, which is not directly contained in the original business requirements, or the project budget. Identify a few team members, who look at web site building as a hobby; it will be easy to talk them into doing this off hours. But don't make the site so simple that it has a homegrown look. Use the latest tools possible. For example instead of just using straight HTML, use tools like Macromedia Flash, Macromedia Dream Weaver, and other products that are associated with cutting edge in the industry.

Sandbox

Although the site is not connected with the project in the business sense, you must still use some quality control. Use a mini Quality Assurance procedure. You don't have to have an elaborate Defect Tracking mechanism in place, but ensure some kind of testing. Test it in more then one browser and platform, but don't go overboard in determining compatibility. Sometimes, even huge enterprise level web sites go beyond reasonable means.

One project I was working on spent thousands of effort hours testing the site on operating systems like Windows 3.1. Determine what operating system and browsers the office uses (most probably there will be more then one) and test for those, even if offsite personal will be accessing your site. You can use this as a leverage to demonstrate your sensitivity to using resources and budget wisely.

Storyboard

Design the site correctly. I personally take charge of this and design the whole site in a storyboard fashion. If you have ever worked with Computer Based Training (CBT) or Web Based Training (WBT), you will know the term. Start with a basic flow chart. Designate a process block as the first page, and then spawn out in a tree. Represent and name each page on your flow chart.

For example, have the Main page drawn at the top of the page, followed by the second level pages that link directly to it, and so on. If you do not have experience in designing CBT or WBT courses, seek out a member who does. It is important for the web architecture to follow smoothly.

Once the flow is completed, you can start the storyboard. Divide the page of a Word document in two by inserting a two-cell table. Designate the left side as the "content" side, and the right side as the "programmer/designer" side. On the left side put down the exact content that the user will see. On the right side, have the exact instructions for the web developer.

For example, on the right side you can have something like, "Welcome to Project Time Machine Web Site. Click here to continue". And on the right side you can explain, "Make the welcome banner red. Make the World Icon hot for link to the Project Status Page." The end user never sees the right side, so you have the freedom to be as descriptive as you want, and write anything that you like. Repeat this process for every page on the site.

Regardless, on how sophisticated you decide on making your site, keep certain quality standards, both aesthetic and technical, in mind. Remember that this site helps you justify your project, and gives you the opportunity to shine, as an EPM should.

CHAPTER TEN

▼

THE PATH

The Extreme Project Manager (EPM) stays at a high level, and understands the big picture, at the same time being able to call the shots like a military commander. However, there are certain things, which can affect the general schedule, and the EPM must be aware of them at a relatively acute level. Particularly, I am referring to Critical Path Method (CPM) and Project Evaluation Review Technique (PERT). The EPM will use these analyses in a slightly different way to stay at a certain level.

Walk the Path

I have faint memories of hearing about CPM and PERT when I was a kid, many years ago. So what are such old ideas doing in the EPM topic? I could say that these are very important methods that every Project manager should know.

But then how would I be any different? And as a Project Manager, you probably know CMP and PERT well anyhow...Right? Well, I will make it worth it for you. In a truly EPM fashion, we will hit on CPM and PERT, in a cursory and a slightly different way, where you can use it just enough to give you some kind of a handle in keeping an eye on scheduling.

CPM lets you see the sequence of events of all the tasks, and the time required. It also shows the earliest finish, earliest start, latest finish, and latest start estimates, so you can see the slack in each of these tasks. You need to know the slack, because if you are seeing a sequence of events, then you are also seeing the dependencies of each of these tasks.

Hence, if you are aware of the slack, then you can get a better idea of the adherence to schedule your project is enjoying. As an EPM, here is a way I found to make this simple: When you make the CPM, do not use sub-tasks. Try and stick to summary tasks. However, unlike the Work Breakdown Structure (WBS), where we used a similar method, you may have to use some of your sub-tasks, depending on the time to completion of that task. For example, if a sub-task takes a long time to complete, and has many dependencies, use it in the CPM.

Look on the Bright Side

Yes, even Project Managers are optimistic, especially EPM's. Although, working with PERT, you have to be both, optimistic and pessimistic. Here is what I mean. Like CPM and WBS, PERT also involves the breaking down of the project into tasks. You then must divide the tasks into three schedule categories, most optimistic finish estimate, and most pessimistic finish estimate, and most likely.

Lets say the task of putting the stealth paint on your time machine is most likely going to take three weeks. You must also then consider what is the longest it will take, and what is the shortest amount of time it will take to apply that paint. For example, five weeks and two weeks, respectively.

Here is the advantage of this method in EPM. You can manipulate your timelines effectively. If you feel that the original schedule is running a bit thin, and the overall project forecast was too optimistic, then you can give the pessimistic estimate a little more weight. For example, in this case, you can assign the timeline of six weeks to the paint job. Then, in the final PERT analysis, you will see the results skewed to a longer forecast.

Here is how an EPM can use the information from PERT analysis. As the project stakeholders are more edgy about technical tasks running over schedule (and rightly so), due to more chances of complications, a project overshooting its schedule due to a paint job will be a lot less painful to the stakeholders. This will allow you to give a lot less explanations, and use your time wisely to deliver the project on time. Of course, as a professional Project Manager, you know that if your project is really in trouble, do not use this technique to hide from reality.

Like I mentioned, you probably know CPM and PERT well. However, if you do not, I encourage you to seek it out and use it in your projects. There are many books and white papers written on it. If you are a traditional

Project Manager, you can use these methods to tell you other important factors in your tasks as well. For example, if you notice the PERT estimates to be off by greater margins, then you must take a closer look at the task, as it is indicating greater risk, then a task that has a smaller spread.

Keep at a high level, and trust your team leads, by delegating the more specific analysis to them. And always remember, if you are an EPM, then use all this information to always show off the project as the greatest thing the client has ever seen.

—————————▼—————————

Chapter Eleven

The Big Breakdown

We construct a Work Breakdown Structure (WBS) on a constant basis in our lives. In fact, nothing is ever done without it. We wake up in the morning, brush our teeth, have breakfast…and so on and so forth, till we meet our final objective, which is to be get dressed in the morning to go to work. In essence, we break down the structure of that one big objective, in small manageable tasks. And that is the definition of WBS, the breakdown of tasks in small manageable portions.

Actually, WBS goes a bit deeper then that. As in most projects, many different groups may come together to form a deliverable. A strong structure is needed. As my Extreme Managers do everything at light speed, the Extreme WBS is broken down to its simplest form, Functional and Chronological. One is chosen as the dominant structure, and the other is chosen as its subset.

Functional WBS structure

If the project is a strong technical project, where many separate development modules will be constructed, then the Functional structure is chosen. The WBS is broken down first by function, then by timeline. Basically, we are giving more importance to the function, then the timeline, as far as the layouts of the tasks are concerned.

Lets assume that you are a Project Manager on a project that will automate the registration of their clients for the training classes, which they offer. The project is going to take 24 months to complete, and will be made up of four fundamental modules. The first module will be the User Interface for the program, for the clients and the administrators. The second module will be an accounts receivable program that will process the payments from the clients. The third module will receive class requests and allocate the schedule. And the forth module will build a web portal for the registration on the company's website.

Each one of these individual modules will have numerous tasks associated with it. In the Functional WBS model, we will list out the four modules, then under each one of those modules, we will list the individual tasks that will make up that particular module, in order of the task's start time. Of course, each task can be further drilled down, to form additional hierarchies. However, in Extreme Management, we sill stop at this level.

Remember the brushing your teeth example? Well, in one of my project management training classes, the instructor gave the example of cleaning the house. He pointed out to make sure that we gave out clear detailed task list. If the task involves the cleaning of the walls, then it must be spelled out that the cleaning of the light switches should be a sub task of that. In our case, we could have indicated that one should pick up the tooth paste, squeeze the paste with a certain amount of pressure (depending on the brand of the tooth paste), dispense a half inch strip on the front side of the tooth brush, and so on, The same could be applied to the WBS for a project. One can go to excruciating details.

Chronological Tree and Trunk

It must be noted that details have their place in Project Management. However, it is not with the Extreme Project Manager; rather, with the specific Team Lead. In Extreme Project Management, the project is executed in a 'lean and mean' manner. Proper delegations must be deployed. If you don't trust your Team Lead with the sub-tasks, replace that lead. The WBS will consist of manageable tasks, but not manageable sub-tasks. Thus, the Extreme WBS structure does not look like a tree, with multiple branches sprouting off their respective multiple branches. But more like a single trunk, with just a few branches sticking out.

The same concept applies to the Chronological structure for the WBS. If the client is very time sensitive, instead of the modules, use timeline, preferably from the original project estimates, to lay out the WBS. Place the module and its subsequent high-level tasks under the timeline, according to the order of their execution. For example, the project may be divided by quarters. Each quarter can have a list of functions under it, in ascending timeline. In the Chronological WBS structure, there will be times, when two or more functions will start at the same time. These functions will have to branch out. Hence, the Chronological WBS structure looks more like a tree, then a trunk.

Client Determination

In the end, strictly maintain the client scope and direction. Determine what is important to the client, the functional perspective for the Functional WBS structure, or the timeline perspective for the Chronological WBS structure. Apply WBS to everything, from the small assignments, to large sub-project applications. Breakdown the tasks in small controllable fragments, and fulfill your objective.

▼

CHAPTER TWELVE

BUDGET UPS AND DOWNS

The Extreme Project Manager (EPM) uses a very clever strategy, when it comes to budgets. The trick is to hold off on the Bottom up Budget, till the very last minute (the actual start of the project), and negotiate with the Top Down Budget. There are many advantages and some challenges with this technique.

Negotiate

There are some fundamentals that one must remember at all times. The Top Down Budget starts from the initial budget that the stakeholder has set aside for the project, and as the name implies, works down to the functions, and then to the tasks. The Bottom Up Budget starts from the tasks, and works its way to the top.

The Bottom Up Budget is considered to be more accurate, and thus exudes more confidence in the stakeholders. Hence, an EPM must put forth the Top Down Budget in front of the stakeholders, and promise the Bottom Up Budget, as soon as the 'experts' are done analyzing all the necessary issues. And as the Top Down Budget is more abstract, it gives the EPM more opportunity to negotiate..

One word of caution here, always remember that things look a lot easier from the top. And I mean that in two ways, the view from the upper management and the view of the Top Down Budget. You may get a hint from the upper management that the budget is way over what they had anticipated. The counter to that is just to quietly remind them of the fact that as the budget gets more 'specific', it gets more complex, and hence takes more resources to complete.

Budget Site

Every EPM knows that you should have a web site dedicated to the project. Budget is something that will highlight it. The Top Down Budget comes in handy here; as it can be broken down in many different categories, which does not necessary follow the Work Breakdown Structure (WBS). A flashy and detailed budget page on the site will give it an air of legitimacy.

It will be helpful to do a little research on this. For example, take a minute to visit other budget sites, such as the site for North Carolina Office of State Budget http://osbpm.state.nc.us/ or the site of the state of Washington's Sate of Financial Management http://www.ofm.wa.gov/budget.htm. Of course, your version will not be as elaborate, or as detailed, but if you use the WBS as a starting point, you can have a pretty convincing budget site. Remember; use the WBS as a guide, not as a template to make the site.

Enterprise Task Model

It is also important to be considering the way your Top Down Budget will be displayed. I use the Enterprise Task Model (ETM). ETM is a high-level view of the summary tasks being used in the project. The format for the enterprise model consists of boxes representing summary tasks. Inside these boxes are smaller boxes representing the tasks, and depending on the complexity of those tasks, further boxes can be illustrated. This gives the audience a glimpse on the relationship of the tasks to the costs, granting your Top Down Budget further validity.

Bottom Up Budget

Although you will be showing the Top Down Budget to everyone, a time will come (sooner then you realize) to introduce the Bottom Down Budget. This budget will have to be as accurate as possible, as it will demand and receive a legitimate amount of acceptance. It has to be accurate, but never under. Hence, you must encourage including every possible contingency in the budget.

To start off the Bottom Down Budget, the first step is to seek out the experts in the particular summary task that need to be budgeted. Be aware that you may need many experts. Do not skimp on these experts; allocate their costs to the planning phase of the project. Advise the experts to consult the documented risks and assumptions to extract the contingencies. Ensure that the contingencies are taken in account both in time and fiscal resources.

Vendor Management

Vendor management is critical whether you are an EPM or a traditional Project Manager. A huge chunk of your budget can disappear on vendors. Vendors can be for anything, from the Internet Service Provider to the janitorial company that empties your wastebaskets at nights. Unfortunately, most vendors are necessary, either the organization cannot produce the necessary resources due to lack of infrastructure, or lacks the essential expertise. Two particular vendor elements that the EPM can control, however, are the rental resources, and consultants.

At times, you will need to rent some equipment. It can be as normal as renting some extra workstations, or as bizarre as renting a 20 foot gorilla. Once, while supervising a grand opening of a huge retail store in Texas, I was required to rent a gigantic gorilla (not a real one) to display on the roof of the store. The cost of the gorilla was about a $1,000 a day, and we wanted it for about a week. With taxes and additional labor to supervise the gorilla, the display would cost the company almost $10,000. Almost all the time, the non-refundable deposit is requested in advance. As an EPM, I negotiated with the vendor for two things, time and money.

The whole price of the resource is not as significant, as the manner in which it is distributed, and the time value is not the total time, but the when it begins.

Our proposal to the company was that we did not have a problem with giving the full asking price, but no payment will be made, till the day of the first rental period. Also, we proposed to the vendor that we could not guarantee the exact start date of the rental, till about a week of the big opening. An important fact to remember is that the later the date of vendor needs, the greater the risk it is to call a specific date. Hence, as the need for the gorilla was at the tail end of our project, the risk was very high that we might not need the gorilla on the exact date scheduled. And as once you part with your money, you immediately loose power in any balance, we thought it was prudent to hold off on the deposit as well.

Another vendor management crucial to supervise properly is the consultants. Every experienced Project Manager will tell you some horror story about how some consulting company nibbled away on the budget, and no productivity was realized. You must understand that it is not the consulting company that devours the resources, but just bad management.

There is not a single reputable consulting company in existence that will force its consultants on you. Sadly, I have been to a lot of projects, where the consultants just sat around, or had some kind of a downtime during the day. At an average of $125 an hour for forty consultants...Well, it s too painful to think about it.

One way to combat consultant downtime is to contract 10% of what you really need. 10% seems like an impossible figure to get the job done, but if you look at the historical data of your own company, or will see that the first few weeks are usually unproductive, due to the logistic concerns and the learning curve.

Once the 10% of the consultants are well settled, then instruct the account executive of the consulting company to filter the rest of the consultants in 10% at a time, to absorb the logistic and the learning shock. It is a lot easier to quickly bring five consultants up to speed, on the job, then fifty.

Necessitate your experts to put everything in writing. This will be your proof that you need a certain amount of resources to meet the fiscal requirements. Employ Technical Writers and Business Analyst to ensure that all the business requirements, assumptions, and risks have been covered.

Budgets are often either the Achilles heel, or the point of glory for the Project Manager. The Bottom Up Budget, which will be the way to go for the final run is more acceptable to the stakeholders, but can be brutal for the Project Manager, if revealed too soon. By maneuvering the

Top Down Budget as long as you can, and managing the vendors properly, the EPM can stay well above the water.

CHAPTER THIRTEEN

▼

WEAPONS FOR THE PROJECT MANAGER

I flew alone over the warm Adriatic Sea. My weapon's bay carried one GBU-10 2000 lbs laser guided bomb. One, because my other bay was occupied by a camera...You see, I was on a reconnaissance mission (so I don't get in trouble, lets just say I was playing a video game). It may seem like a far cry, but the Extreme Project Manager also has weapons. You can kill with them, use them to help people, and you can manipulate situations with them. And just like the plane that I was flying, there is a limit on what the Extreme Project Manager (EPM) can carry.

Do not confuse weapons with tools. A weapon is used to contend against an opponent. A tool is used to complete a task. For example, Microsoft Project is a tool, while Change Control is a weapon. The EPM will use the tool, and create the weapon. However, only a few tools must be used at a time, otherwise you will overwhelm the client, and your project staff.

For example, Change Control requires forms to be filled out, information to be channeled interdepartmentally, control numbers to be assigned,
scope creep data to be managed and tracked, and so forth. In other words,
each weapon that you create will generate some extra work for the project
staff.

Many people are slightly taken aback by the confrontational nature of
Extreme Project Management. It really is not confrontational at all. In
fact, it is designed to avoid confrontations before it is realized. It keeps the
EPM two steps ahead at all times of everybody else.

Change Control

Our first and the most important weapon is Change Control. We will start with Change Management, as I am always fighting about it in virtually every project that I do. In Change Control, our primary objective is to combat scope creep. Scope creep is the steady addition of requirements, which were not stated originally.

The process of Change Control starts with the person making the change. This person is usually on the business side (or whichever side that owns/initiates the project). The change initiator fills out a form, which is passed along to the team lead of the module/function being affected. Once the change seems technologically feasible and makes business sense, it is passed along to the project manager. At this point, the team lead and Project Manager decide how much time should be added to the project, or how much money should be added to the budget to add the necessary resources (or both).

Once this decision is made, the project manager signs the form and the form is forwarded to the person, who originally initiated the change. The originator's department then approves the increase in the resources, and the change is created, by assigning it a control number.

There are some documents that power Change Control. The first is the Change Control Form, which is created in MS Word. The form must have enough entries to identify the change in detail, the possible impact on the technological and the business sides, and spaces for remarks and signatures. The second piece of document is the Change Control Tracking Database, which is created in MS Access. The database mirrors the Ms Word form exactly. The database is updated every time a control number is assigned.

Issue Control

Issue Control is a bit simpler then Change Control. The Issue Control is charged primarily with the Issue list. The Issue list is basically made up of defect that can be put aside for further discussion between the stakeholders and the EPM, for a latter date. Usually, non-critical defects, which do not make the Change Control list, end up in Issue Control.

Similar to the Change Control, Issue Control must be managed professionally by the EPM. The two documents needed for proper Issue Control are the Issue Control Form, and the Issue Tracking Database. The rite of passage to Issue Control is a bit different.

It is recommended that the forms and the tracking styles are purposely made different to avoid confusion, as a lot of information in the forms and the tracking databases may seem similar. Also, the numbering system in Issue Control is slightly different. Whenever a defect is not fixed, and moved off to a "holding area" somewhere, the stakeholders get a little nervous about the future of that defect. Because of this reason, the Issue number is the same as the Defect Number. This is done to avoid 'misplacing' any defects.

Cloud Surprise

Okay, I am going to push the envelope a bit here. This is where we become "extreme" and sometimes get into trouble. But it is worth it. Cloud Surprise is a weapon that is more psychological then functional. But it is incredibly effective every time it is used.

Cloud Surprise is a pretense, which is unleashed on the victim to dampened bad news, amplify good news, or simply to color dull news.

It will be interesting to declare how I came up with the term, Cloud Surprise. Then you will understand the reason for its existence.

A few years ago, I used to fly with a friend of mine, who was quite a daring pilot. Although I avoid roller coasters, I am quite an excitement junkie, when it comes to flying. Cloud Surprise basically entailed us flying straight into the clouds from the bottom, till we broke free on the other side...All of a sudden being blinded by the bright sunlight; or, sharply diving from the top till we broke out from the clouds, and saw the ground approaching at a high speed, to fill our view inside the cockpit.

Although we knew exactly what lied on the other side, it was kind of a surprise to see the bright sunshine, or the approaching ground. We were so engrossed in speeding through the clouds, and having a strong feeling of anxiety and apprehension that our knowledge of what lied on the other side was temporarily forgotten: hence, the name Cloud Surprise.

I use this weapon when I have to deliver news, which the staff is expecting, but not necessary with great anticipation. For example, when I have to inform the IT staff that they will have to work on New Year's Eve to monitor the network, I would first indicate to them that they may all have to work a 12 hour shift, maybe even 16. I usually qualify this statement by adding a bit of detail to it, such as advising them to wear comfortable clothes, and to charge their cell phones. Then a few hours before the shift,

I will proclaim that they only, in fact, have to be there for a four-hour period, just to monitor the change of date. This is usually met with cheers of happiness! Get the idea? Cloud Surprise!

Counter-surveillance

Keep your ears open. There is no need to actually spy on your coworkers. An EPM keeps all issues at a high level, delegating authority to the appropriate staff members. Hence, small details should be left to the team leads. However, it does not hurt to be informed. If you spot two people, who are sensitive to your project, having a conversion, casually walk within earshot, and do some simple task, like tying your shoelaces, or pretending to have a conversation with another coworker.

Keep your eyes open too. Carefully check out everything that goes within your range of vision. Documents are very powerful. Many companies go to great lengths to ensure that the right people look at the right things. For example, Motorola has a whole methodology on how statuses are assigned to the documents in the hierarchy of privacy, and how the employees handle those documents.

In general, be aware of everything that goes around you in the organization. This may seem like a frivolous advice. But by trying a bit harder and practicing surveillance techniques, you will have a fantastic advantage over the rest of the managers.

The use of some of these weapons may sound a bit draconian, but they work. And remember the final objective of an EPM is the greatness of the project for your client, and even a superior greatness for you.

CHAPTER FOURTEEN

———————▼———————

THE UNSTOPPABLE FIGHTING MACHINE

Being an Extreme Project Manager is like being an unstoppable fighting machine, you eliminate all the obstacles in your way efficiently and effectively, at the same time generating the results for the project, which are beyond expectations.

Being an EPM is not for everybody, but can be, by following certain easy to follow, yet unique, methodologies. You certainly have to be a superior individual to become an EPM, and continue to maintain the practice. However, one of the prerequisites to becoming a superior Project Manager is first to be an average one. To become a full-fledged EPM, one must follow some fundamental rules. For the last few years, I have been closely watching some very good Project Managers, and here are some of the things I picked out.

Manage and Track

Manage, but do not micro-manage. Delegate as much authority as you feel comfortable with, in fact, reach out of your comfort zone, and have confidence in your staff. Do not thrust your ideas on your team leads to follow, but rather suggest it to them. Explicitly express this to them by asking for their opinion first. Keep in mind the Side Alpha-Side Bravo concept from the Meetings chapter. It is always nice to have a spare brain.

Not micro-managing does not mean managing loosely. Track the status of the team leads carefully. Do not attempt to track the status of everyone in your staff. Let your team leads do that. Be cautious of over tracking. The best way is to have a Technical Writer or a Business Analyst come up with simple criteria to track, and assign that person around five to ten hours a week to be the administrator of tracking these criteria. Encourage the use of simple tools like MS Word or MS Excel to generate high-level charts to minimize your time for studying this information.

Counterattack and Mediate

There may me certain times, when one of your staff members may cross the line, and either question your authority, or merely imply that you lack certain technical virtues. This is very common in IT organizations. The attacking member may have a certain truth in it, as you can never know everything about everything. However, never tolerate mutiny. Do whatever it takes to reassign the employee to a different group. Even an average Project Manager knows that the staff must respect the authority.

Never let a confrontation between your staff members escalate to an uncomfortable level. Immediately intervene and curtly ask for the disagreement to be taken 'offline'. Be acutely aware of any past disagreement that may exist between team members. In a subtle way, keep reminding everyone that only team players are needed in the group. Deal with troubled employees swiftly. Once again, council the appropriate team leads to tackle the employee.

Use Tools

Learn how to use common management tools, and especially know all the common tools, such as provided in MS Office Suites. If you do not like Microsoft products, be familiar with it anyway. In fact, be familiar with all the common tools used in the office environment, such as FrameMaker. Visio, and other applications used in day-to-day activities. Learn to use MS Project well. The reports it generates, and the tracking options it offers, are invaluable.

In the end, strive to be an EPM. It may sound like a cliché, but practice will guide toward perfection. An EPM's results are astounding, however, the means are subtle. This requires the Project Manager to have the strength of a superior leader; at the same time have the finesse and refinement of a great actor. The best thing you can do is to bring all the methodology and skills of the Extreme Project Manager together, and just apply in your work. It is unbelievably satisfying to actually enjoy the process of being an EPM, at the same time reap the rewards of the generated consequences.

0-595-21335-9